Plastic Canvas Spinners™

Designs by Janelle Giese

Contents

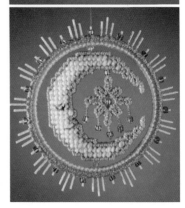

General Instructions

Stitching Step by Step

Cutting

1 Cut central motifs from clear plastic canvas according to graph(s) and instructions for individual design. *Note: For the Hearts Spinner only, the central motif is cut from white 7-count plastic canvas. For the Cross Spinner only, the central motif is cut from almond plastic canvas.*

2 For beaded edging strip, cut one piece according to graph from white or almond 7-count plastic canvas, according to instructions for individual design.

3 For spinner's outer ring, cut away the inner portion from both 4-inch plastic canvas circles, leaving the outermost rings 1 hole wide.

4 Cut any other pieces from 7-count plastic canvas according to instructions for individual design.

Central Motif

1 Referring to color key and graph(s) for individual design throughout, work the background stitching on the central motif and any other 7-count plastic canvas pieces. Stitch the pieces exactly as graphed. Do not carry the fiber over the cut corners of the plastic canvas; these must remain open for joining.

2 Add embroidery stitches and any bead clusters (see below).

- *Adding bead clusters*: Thread a beading needle with bead thread; knot the end. Anchor the thread in the stitching on the wrong side with a Backstitch. Draw the needle through to the front at a bead cluster placement point. Thread three beads onto needle according to instructions for individual design. Take the needle back down at the same point and draw the thread taut, forming a cluster of three beads. Repeat to add bead clusters at remaining bead placement points. Knot the thread on the back of the work; draw the thread tail through stitches on the wrong side and trim.

3 Whipstitch central motifs together, wrong sides facing. As you stitch, check both sides for even coverage, and to make sure that the embroidery stitches are not caught under the Whipstitching.

Outer Ring

Holding the two plastic canvas rings together, Whipstitch the beaded edging strip to the rings along the outer edge, working through all layers. The bars of the beaded edging strip will not align perfectly with the bars of the rings.

- To ensure correct spacing of pebble beads, make sure that the beaded edging strip rests outside the outer bars of the circle, and that the Whipstitches run as straight up and down as possible.

- To ensure even coverage on front and back, stitches to cover the extended bars on the beaded edging strip may "lean" in one direction or another. If the stitches are correct, the ends of the beaded edging strip will overlap by about one hole's width. If the stitches are more angled, there will be a larger overlap, which will position the last bead on the edging strip too close to the adjacent group of three plastic canvas bars.

- To more easily begin and end stitching with the lengths of metallic braid when Whipstitching the beaded edging strip to the rings, begin by cutting one 1-yard (0.9m) and two 1½-yard (14m) lengths of metallic braid in the color specified by the instructions for the individual design. Using any of the three pieces, begin Whipstitching as described in step 1. As you near the end of the first length, position the end of the second length against the ring and conceal it under the final stitches taken with the first length. When you reach the end of the first length, remove the needle; thread the second length onto the needle, and continue stitching, concealing the end of the first length under these stitches. Continue stitching, then finish off the second length and add the third in the same manner. At the end of the third length of braid, you will have only one end of braid to conceal. Thread the final end of the third fiber onto a smaller tapestry needle and draw it through completed stitches.

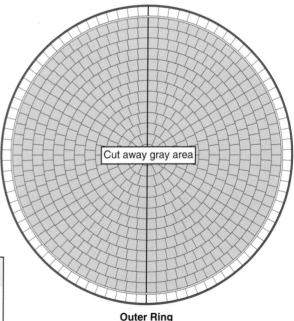

Cut away gray area

Outer Ring
Cut 2 from 4-inch plastic canvas circles for each design

Key for Outer Ring & Beaded Edging	
■	Heavy (#32) Braid
☐	Plastic canvas yarn
✎	Attach bead

Assembly

1 Position the ring so that the overlapped ends of the beaded edging strip are near the bottom of the spinner and a bead placement bar is at the very top. *(Bead placement bars are highlighted in red on the graph for the Beaded Edging Strip.)*

2 Referring to the center arrows on the graph for the individual design, insert a doll needle into the top center point of the central motif. Draw the needle down between the joined halves until it protrudes from the bottom center point of the motif. Set the piece aside with the doll needle in place.

3 Cut a generous length of clear monofilament thread, long enough so that it can be doubled and still extend a few inches beyond the perimeter of the ring. Knot the center of the clear thread to the unworked bar of plastic canvas on the inside of the ring at the very top of the ring *(directly below a beaded bar)*.

4 Thread both ends of the clear thread into the correct needle as directed in individual instructions; string on beads as instructed.

5 Remove the thread ends from the needle without letting beads slip off. Thread the thread ends through the eye of the doll needle in the plastic canvas motif. Pull the needle through the plastic canvas motif.

6 At the bottom of the plastic canvas motif, thread the ends of the clear thread onto the same needle used in step 4. Thread on beads as instructed.

7 Attach and knot the ends of the clear thread onto the inner edge of the ring at the bottom of the spinner, tightening the thread so as to secure it without distorting the shape of the ring.

Finishing

1 Overcast along the inner edge of the ring using yarn as directed in the instructions for the individual design. Begin by weaving the yarn tail over three bars of plastic canvas. This will hold the first stitch at the proper angle. Continue overcasting around the ring. When nearing the end, work over the yarn tail, concealing it under the final stitches. Draw the end of the working yarn through stitching; trim both tails.

2 Using clear monofilament thread, knot a 4-inch hanging loop around the outermost bar at the very top of the ring.

3 Using a cotton-tipped swab, apply glue to bead placement bars; slide a pebble bead onto each. Before sliding the pebble bead onto the glued bar at the top of the spinner, draw the hanging loop through the bead.

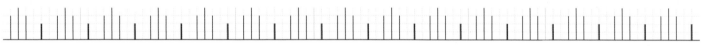

Beaded Edging
90 holes x 4 holes
Cut 1 for each spinner from white or almond plastic canvas,
according to instructions for individual design;
cut away blue lines

Butterfly

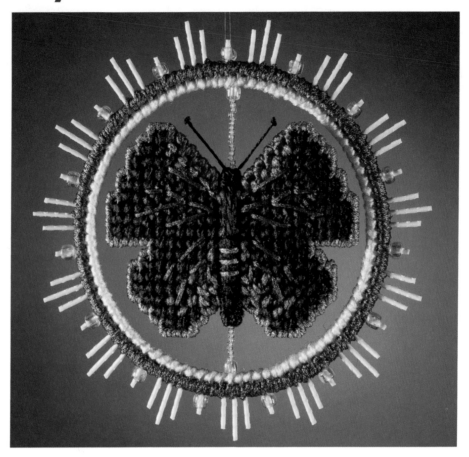

Size: 5½ inches (14cm) in diameter
Skill Level: Intermediate

Materials

- ❑ 7-count plastic canvas:
    - ¼ sheet clear
    - 90 x 4-hole strip white
- ❑ 2 (4-inch) plastic canvas circles
- ❑ Uniek Needloft plastic canvas yarn as listed in color key
- ❑ Kreinik Heavy (#32) Braid as listed in color key
- ❑ DMC size 5 pearl cotton as listed in color key
- ❑ Clear monofilament thread
- ❑ Mill Hill glass pebble beads:
    - 17 crystal #05161
- ❑ Mill Hill glass seed beads:
    - 25 crystal #00161
- ❑ #16 tapestry needle
- ❑ Beading needle
- ❑ 4-inch (10.2cm) or longer doll needle
- ❑ Cotton-tipped swab
- ❑ Thick white craft glue

Stitching Step by Step

Cutting

1 Cut two butterflies from clear plastic canvas according to graph.

2 Cut beaded edging strip from white plastic canvas; cut plastic canvas circles to form rings.

Central Motif

1 Work Continental Stitches on both butterflies according to graphs, filling in uncoded areas with dark royal Continental Stitches.

2 Embroider wings as follows:

Black size 5 pearl cotton—Backstitch on top of purple Continental Stitches.
Sky blue heavy (#32) braid—Backstitch on top of royal Continental Stitches according to graph.
Blue heavy (#32) braid—Straight Stitch accents on wings.

3 Work body as follows, referring to Butterfly Body Detail graph:

Black yarn—Work the shorter vertical Straight Stitches, then the longer Straight Stitch in the center.

Black size 5 pearl cotton—Work the top horizontal stitch around the vertical Straight Stitches, drawing pearl cotton to front of motif at center; wrap pearl cotton around vertical yarn stitches and go back down through same point, gathering the yarn stitches slightly. Work the bottom two horizontal Straight Stitches over the vertical yarn stitches.

Sky blue heavy (#32) braid—Work the remaining horizontal Straight Stitches on top of the vertical yarn stitches.

4 Whipstitch the butterflies together using black and royal yarns and sky blue heavy (#32) braid according to graph.

5 *Form antennae*: Knot one end of a length of black size 5 pearl cotton. Draw opposite end through top of head just below the Whipstitched edge. Knot and trim the end of the pearl cotton, then adjust length so antennae are even. Moisten your fingers with a few drops of craft glue; run your fingers over the antennae to stiffen them.

Outer Ring

Join the white beaded edging strip to the rings using blue heavy (#32) braid.

Assembly

Suspend the butterfly in the ring, threading one crystal pebble bead and 16 crystal seed beads onto the clear thread at the top of the butterfly, and nine crystal seed beads and one crystal pebble bead at the bottom of the butterfly.

Finishing

1 Overcast the inner edge of the ring using white yarn.

2 Attach hanging loop.

3 Glue a crystal pebble bead to each bead placement bar on the edging strip, drawing the hanging loop through the pebble bead at the top of the *spinner*.

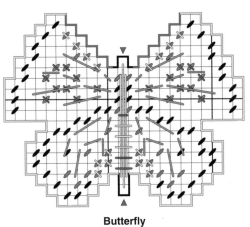

Butterfly
23 holes x 18 holes
Cut 2 from clear plastic canvas

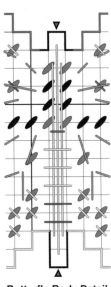

Butterfly Body Detail

COLOR KEY

Yards	Plastic Canvas Yarn
4 (3.7m)	■ Black #00
2 (1.8m)	■ Royal #32
2 (1.8m)	White #41
1 (0.9m)	■ Purple #46
5 (4.6m)	Uncoded areas on butterfly are dark royal #48 Continental Stitches
	⁄ Black #00 Straight Stitch
Heavy (#32) Braid	
6 (5.5m)	⁄ Blue #006 Straight Stitch
4 (3.7m)	⁄ Sky blue #014 Backstitch, Straight Stitch and Whipstitch
Size 5 Pearl Cotton	
4 (3.7m)	⁄ Black #310 Backstitch and Straight Stitch

Color numbers given are for Uniek Needloft plastic canvas yarn, Kreinik Heavy (#32) Braid and DMC size 5 pearl cotton.

Ladybug

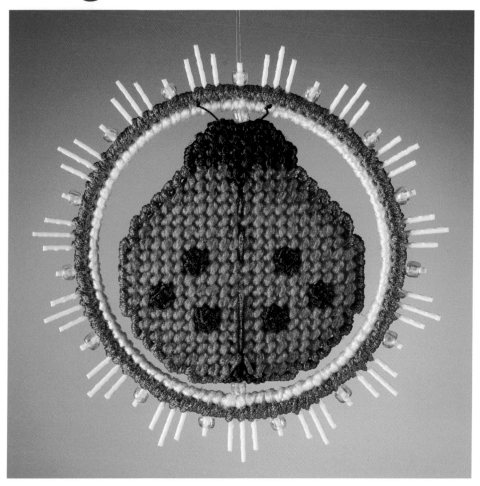

Size: 5½ inches (14cm) in diameter
Skill Level: Intermediate

Materials

- ❏ 7-count plastic canvas:
    ¼ sheet clear
    90 x 4-hole strip white
- ❏ 2 (4-inch) plastic canvas circles
- ❏ Uniek Needloft plastic canvas yarn as listed in color key
- ❏ Kreinik Heavy (#32) Braid as listed in color key
- ❏ DMC size 8 pearl cotton as listed in color key
- ❏ Clear monofilament thread
- ❏ Mill Hill glass pebble beads:
    17 crystal #05161
- ❏ #16 tapestry needle
- ❏ 4-inch (10.2cm) or longer doll needle
- ❏ Cotton-tipped swab
- ❏ Thick white craft glue

Stitching Step by Step

Cutting

1 Cut two ladybugs from clear plastic canvas according to graph.

2 Cut beaded edging strip from white plastic canvas; cut plastic canvas circles to form rings.

Central Motif

1 Stitch both ladybugs according to graph, filling in uncoded areas with Christmas red Continental Stitches.

2 When the background stitching is complete, add embroidery stitches as follows:

Red heavy (#32) braid—Backstitch and Straight Stitch accents down center, under head, and at bottom.
Black size 8 pearl cotton—Backstitch and Straight Stitch details next to red heavy (#32) braid stitches.

3 Whipstitch the ladybugs together using black yarn and red heavy (#32) braid according to graph.

4 *Form antennae*: Knot one end of a length of black size 8 pearl cotton. Draw opposite end through top of head just below the Whipstitched edge. Knot and trim the end of the pearl cotton, then adjust length so antennae are even. Moisten your fingers with a few drops of craft glue; run your fingers over the antennae to stiffen them.

Outer Ring

Join the white beaded edging strip to the rings using red heavy (#32) braid.

Assembly

Suspend the ladybug in the ring, threading one crystal pebble bead onto the clear thread at the top of the ladybug, and one at the bottom of the ladybug.

Finishing

1 Overcast the inner edge of the ring using white yarn.

2 Attach hanging loop.

3 Glue a crystal pebble bead to each bead placement bar on the edging strip, drawing the hanging loop through the pebble bead at the top of the spinner.

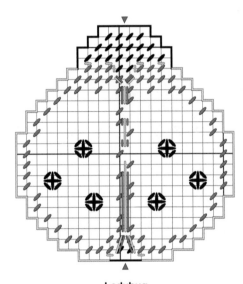

Ladybug
21 holes x 22 holes
Cut 2 from clear plastic canvas

COLOR KEY		
Yards	**Plastic Canvas Yarn**	
3 (2.7m)	■ Black #00	
3 (2.7m)	■ Red #01	
2 (1.8m)	White #41	
6 (5.5m)	Uncoded areas on ladybug are Christmas red #02 Continental Stitches	
	Heavy (#32) Braid	
8 (7.3m)	⁄ Red #003 Backstitch and Straight Stitch	
	Size 8 Pearl Cotton	
1 (0.9m)	⁄ Black #310 Backstitch and Straight Stitch	
Color numbers given are for Uniek Needloft plastic canvas yarn; Kreinik Heavy (#32) Braid and DMC size 8 pearl cotton.		

Bee

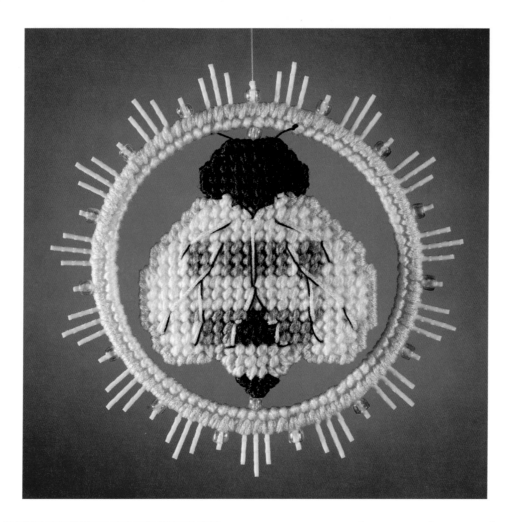

Size: 5½ inches (14cm) in diameter
Skill Level: Intermediate

Materials

❏ 7-count plastic canvas:
    ¼ sheet clear
    90 x 4-hole strip white
❏ 2 (4-inch) plastic canvas circles
❏ Uniek Needloft plastic canvas yarn as listed in color key
❏ Kreinik Heavy (#32) Braid as listed in color key
❏ DMC size 8 pearl cotton as listed in color key
❏ Clear monofilament thread
❏ Mill Hill glass pebble beads:
    17 crystal #05161
❏ #16 tapestry needle
❏ 4-inch (10.2cm) or longer doll needle
❏ Cotton-tipped swab
❏ Thick white craft glue

Stitching Step by Step

Cutting

1 Cut two bees from clear plastic canvas according to graph.

2 Cut beaded edging strip from white plastic canvas; cut plastic canvas circles to form rings.

Central Motif

1 Stitch both bees according to graph, filling in uncoded areas with white Continental Stitches.

2 When the background stitching is complete, add embroidery stitches as follows:

Pearl heavy (#32) braid—Backstitch and Straight Stitch body and wings.
Black size 8 pearl cotton—Backstitch and Straight Stitch remaining details on body and wings.

3 Whipstitch the bees together using black and yellow yarns and pearl heavy (#32) braid according to graph.

4 *Form antennae*: Knot one end of a length of black size 8 pearl cotton. Draw opposite end through top of head just below the Whipstitched edge. Knot and trim the end of the pearl cotton, then adjust length so antennae are even. Moisten your fingers with a few drops of craft glue; run your fingers over the antennae to stiffen them.

Outer Ring

Join the white beaded edging strip to the rings using sunlight heavy (#32) braid.

Assembly

Suspend the bee in the ring, threading one crystal pebble bead onto the clear thread at the top of the bee, and one at the bottom of the *bee*.

Finishing

1 Overcast the inner edge of the ring using white yarn.

2 Attach hanging loop.

3 Glue a crystal pebble bead to each bead placement bar on the edging strip, drawing the hanging loop through the pebble bead at the top of the spinner.

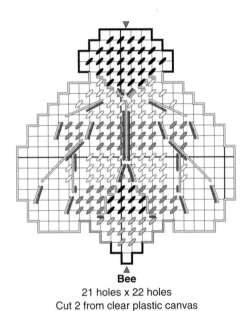

Bee
21 holes x 22 holes
Cut 2 from clear plastic canvas

COLOR KEY		
Yards	**Plastic Canvas Yarn**	
3 (2.7m)	■	Black #00
2 (1.8m)	□	Baby yellow #21
2 (1.8m)	▨	Gray #38
1 (0.9m)	▨	Yellow #57
6 (5.5m)		Uncoded areas on bee are white #41 Continental Stitches
Heavy (#32) Braid		
4 (3.7m)	✎	Pearl #032 Backstitch, Straight Stitch and Whipstitch
4 (3.7m)		Sunlight #9100
Size 8 Pearl Cotton		
2 (1.8m)	✎	Black #310 Backstitch and Straight Stitch

Color numbers given are for Uniek Needloft plastic canvas yarn, Kreinik Heavy (#32) Braid and DMC size 8 pearl cotton.

Birdhouse

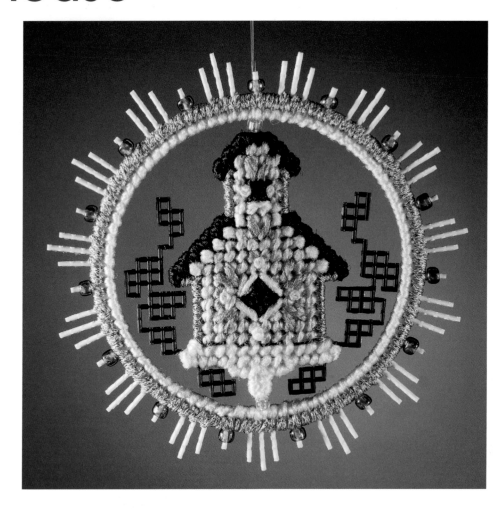

Size: 5½ inches (14cm) in diameter
Skill Level: Intermediate

Materials

- 7-count plastic canvas:
    - ¼ sheet clear
    - ¼ sheet dark green
    - 90 x 4-hole strip white
- 2 (4-inch) plastic canvas circles
- Uniek Needloft plastic canvas yarn as listed in color key
- Kreinik Heavy (#32) Braid as listed in color key
- DMC size 5 pearl cotton as listed in color key
- 2 yards (1.8m) bead thread
- Clear monofilament thread
- White sewing thread (optional)
- Mill Hill glass pebble beads:
    - 2 crystal #05161
    - 15 amethyst #05202
- #16 tapestry needle
- 4-inch (10.2cm) or longer doll needle
- Hand-sewing needle (optional)
- Cotton-tipped swab
- Thick white craft glue

Stitching Step by Step

Cutting

1 Cut two birdhouses from clear plastic canvas and one birdhouse vines section from dark green plastic canvas according to graphs.

2 Cut beaded edging strip from white plastic canvas; cut plastic canvas circles to form rings.

Central Motif

1 Stitch both birdhouses according to graph, filling in uncoded areas with orchid Continental Stitches.

2 When the background stitching is complete, add embroidery stitches as follows:

Black yarn—Referring to stitch diagram below, work Smyrna Cross Stitches in door and at top of birdhouse.

White yarn—Straight Stitch outline around door and across base of smaller opening at top; work French Knot perch at base of door, wrapping yarn around needle once.

Lavender yarn—Straight Stitch V-shaped "hearts."

1 ply separated from a strand of fern yarn—Backstitch leaves.

1 ply separated from a strand of yellow yarn—Work French Knot flowers, wrapping yarn around needle twice.

Ultra dark beaver gray size 5 pearl cotton—Backstitch and Straight Stitch remaining details.

3 Sandwich vines section between stitched birdhouses, aligning Whipstitching lines highlighted in red across bottom of birdhouses and on vines section. Whipstitch to join all layers along these lines using white yarn.

4 Finish Whipstitching birdhouses together along edges using white and black yarns and rose quartz heavy (#32) braid, according to graph.

Option: *After joining, the vines may want to lean outward. To remedy this, secure them to the birdhouse with a few tiny stitches at tack points indicated by red dots on graph using a sewing needle and white sewing thread.*

Outer Ring

Join the white beaded edging strip to the rings using rose quartz heavy (#32) braid.

Assembly

Suspend the birdhouse in the ring, threading one crystal pebble bead onto the clear thread at the top of the birdhouse, and one at the bottom of the birdhouse.

Finishing

1 Overcast the inner edge of the ring using white yarn.

2 Attach hanging loop.

3 Glue an amethyst pebble bead to each bead placement bar on the edging strip, drawing the hanging loop through the pebble bead at the top of the spinner.

Birdhouse
15 holes x 22 holes
Cut 2 from clear plastic canvas

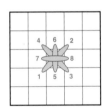

Smyrna Cross Stitch
Bring needle up at odd numbers and down at even numbers

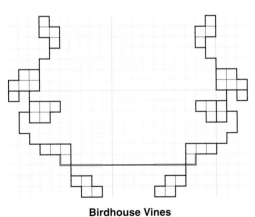

Birdhouse Vines
23 holes x 17 holes
Cut 1 from dark green plastic canvas,
cutting away blue lines

COLOR KEY	
Yards	**Plastic Canvas Yarn**
2 (1.8m)	■ Black #00
1 (0.9m)	▨ Fern #23
5 (4.6m)	□ White #41
3 (2.7m)	Uncoded areas on birdhouse are orchid #44 Continental Stitches
1 (0.9m)	✴ Black #00 Smyrna Cross Stitch
	∕ Fern #23 1-ply Backstitch
	∕ Lavender #05 Straight Stitch
1 (0.9m)	∕ White #41 Straight Stitch
	○ White #41 French Knot (1 wrap)
	○ Yellow #57 1-ply French Knot (2 wraps)
	Heavy (#32) Braid
4 (3.7m)	∕ Rose quartz #3237 Whipstitch
	Size 5 Pearl Cotton
1 (0.9m)	∕ Ultra dark beaver gray #844 Backstitch and Straight Stitch
	∕ Whipstitch line
	● Tack point

Color numbers given are for Uniek Needloft plastic canvas yarn, Kreinik Heavy (#32) Braid and DMC size 5 pearl cotton.

Blue Jay

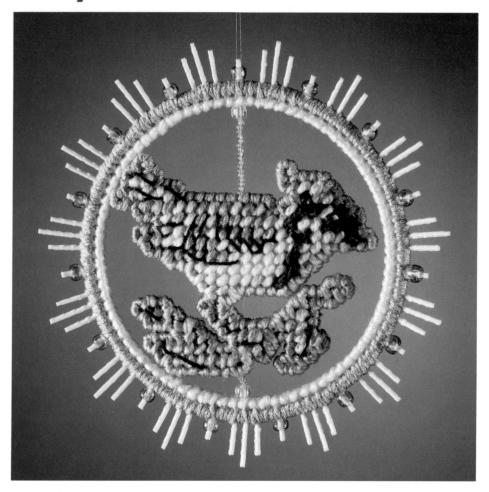

Size: 5½ inches (14cm) in diameter
Skill Level: Intermediate

Materials

❑ 7-count plastic canvas:
  ¼ sheet clear
  90 x 4-hole strip white
❑ 2 (4-inch) plastic canvas circles
❑ Uniek Needloft plastic canvas yarn as listed in color key
❑ Kreinik Heavy (#32) Braid as listed in color key
❑ DMC size 5 pearl cotton as listed in color key
❑ Clear monofilament thread
❑ Mill Hill glass seed beads:
  22 crystal #00161
❑ Mill Hill glass pebble beads:
  2 crystal #05161
  15 sapphire #05168
❑ #16 tapestry needle
❑ Beading needle
❑ 4-inch (10.2cm) or longer doll needle
❑ Cotton-tipped swab
❑ Thick white craft glue

Stitching Step by Step

Cutting

1 Cut one blue jay A and one blue jay B from clear plastic canvas according to graphs.

2 Cut beaded edging strip from white plastic canvas; cut plastic canvas circles to form rings.

Central Motif

1 Stitch both blue jays according to graph, filling in uncoded areas with sail blue Continental Stitches.

2 When the background stitching is complete, add embroidery stitches as follows:

Black yarn—Straight Stitch details on head and chest; work French Knot eyes, wrapping yarn around needle once

1 ply separated from a strand of white yarn—Backstitch a tiny highlight in each eye.

Black size 5 pearl cotton—Backstitch and Straight Stitch remaining details on head, beak, wings, tail and leaves.

3 Whipstitch the blue jays together using sandstone, moss, silver and gray yarns and periwinkle heavy (#32) braid, according to graphs.

Outer Ring

Join the white beaded edging strip to the rings using periwinkle heavy (#32) braid.

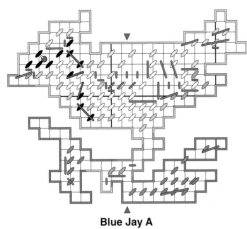

Blue Jay A
23 holes x 18 holes
Cut 1 from clear plastic canvas

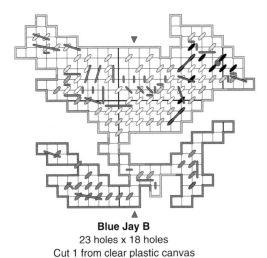

Blue Jay B
23 holes x 18 holes
Cut 1 from clear plastic canvas

Assembly

Suspend the blue jay in the ring, threading one crystal pebble bead and 18 crystal seed beads onto the clear thread at the top of the blue jay, and four crystal seed beads and one crystal pebble bead at the bottom of the blue jay.

Finishing

1 Overcast the inner edge of the ring using white yarn.

2 Attach hanging loop.

3 Glue a sapphire pebble bead to each bead placement bar on the edging strip, drawing the hanging loop through the pebble bead at the top of the spinner.

COLOR KEY	
Yards	**Plastic Canvas Yarn**
1 (0.9m)	■ Black #00
1 (0.9m)	▨ Sandstone #16
2 (1.8m)	▨ Moss #25
1 (0.9m)	☐ Baby blue #36
2 (1.8m)	▨ Silver #37
2 (1.8m)	▨ Gray #38
4 (3.7m)	☐ White #41
2 (1.8m)	Uncoded areas on blue jays are sail blue #57 Continental Stitches
	✎ Black #00 Straight Stitch
	● Black #00 French Knot (1 wrap)
	✎ White #41 1-ply Backstitch
Heavy (#32) Braid	
5 (4.6m)	✎ Periwinkle #9294 Whipstitch
Size 5 Pearl Cotton	
2 (1.8m)	✎ Black #310 Backstitch and Straight Stitch
Color numbers given are for Uniek Needloft plastic canvas yarn, Kreinik Heavy (#32) Braid and DMC size 5 pearl cotton.	

Fish

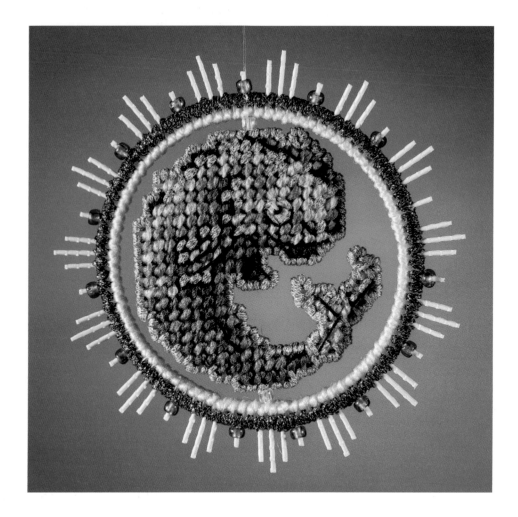

Size: 5½ inches (14cm) in diameter
Skill Level: Intermediate

Materials

❑ 7-count plastic canvas:
   ¼ sheet clear
   90 x 4-hole strip almond
❑ 2 (4-inch) plastic canvas circles
❑ Uniek Needloft plastic canvas yarn as listed in color key
❑ Kreinik Heavy (#32) Braid as listed in color key
❑ DMC size 5 pearl cotton as listed in color key
❑ Clear monofilament thread
❑ Mill Hill glass pebble beads:
   2 crystal #05161
   15 bottle green #05270MH
❑ #16 tapestry needle
❑ 4-inch (10.2cm) or longer doll needle
❑ Cotton-tipped swab
❑ Thick white craft glue

Stitching Step by Step

Cutting

1 Cut one fish A and one fish B from clear plastic canvas according to graphs.

2 Cut beaded edging strip from almond plastic canvas; cut plastic canvas circles to form rings.

Central Motif

1 Stitch both fish according to graphs, filling in uncoded areas with moss Continental Stitches.

2 When the background stitching is complete, embroider eye as follows, referring to Fish Eye Detail graph:

Beige yarn—vertical and horizontal Backstitches.
Black size 5 pearl cotton—Work French Knot in center, wrapping pearl cotton around needle twice.
1 ply separated from a strand of beige yarn—Work diagonal Backstitches between points of previous beige Backstitches.
1 ply separated from a strand of white yarn—Backstitch a tiny highlight in each eye.

Peridot heavy (#32) braid—Work diagonal Backstitches outside diagonal beige yarn Backstitches.

Black size 5 pearl cotton—Work diagonal Backstitches outside bottom two diagonal peridot heavy (#32) braid Backstitches.

3 Backstitch and Straight Stitch remaining details using black size 5 pearl cotton according to fish graphs.

4 Whipstitch the fish together using peridot heavy (#32) braid.

Outer Ring

Join the almond beaded edging strip to the rings using mallard heavy (#32) braid.

Assembly

Suspend the fish in the ring, threading one crystal pebble bead onto the clear thread at the top of the fish, and one at the bottom of the fish.

Finishing

1 Overcast the inner edge of the ring using eggshell yarn.

2 Attach hanging loop.

3 Glue a bottle green pebble bead to each bead placement bar on the edging strip, drawing the hanging loop through the pebble bead at the top of the spinner.

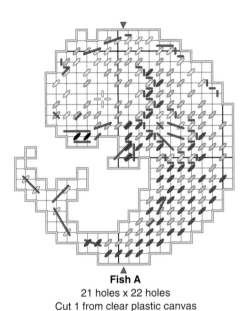

Fish A
21 holes x 22 holes
Cut 1 from clear plastic canvas

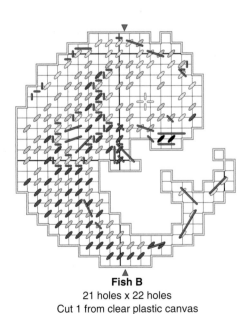

Fish B
21 holes x 22 holes
Cut 1 from clear plastic canvas

COLOR KEY

Yards	Plastic Canvas Yarn
1 (0.9m)	■ Black #00
4 (3.7m)	Christmas green #28
2 (1.8m)	■ Forest #29
2 (1.8m)	Eggshell #39
2 (1.8m)	Uncoded areas on fish are moss #25 Continental Stitches
1 (0.9m)	╱ Beige #40 full-strand Backstitch
	╱ Beige #40 1-ply Backstitch
1 (0.9m)	╱ White #41 1-ply Backstitch
	Heavy (#32) Braid
4 (3.7m)	Mallard #850
8 (7.3m)	☐ Peridot #3215
	╱ Peridot #3215 Backstitch
	Size 5 Pearl Cotton
4 (3.7m)	╱ Black #310 Backstitch and Straight Stitch
	● Black #310 French Knot (2 wraps)

Color numbers given are for Uniek Needloft plastic canvas yarn, Kreinik Heavy (#32) Braid and DMC size 5 pearl cotton.

Fish Eye Detail

Flower

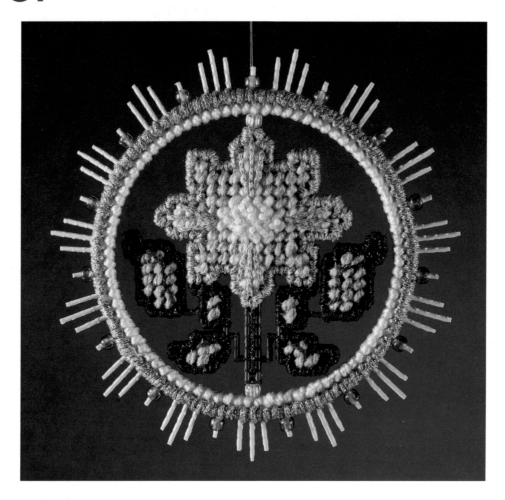

Size: 5½ inches (14cm) in diameter
Skill Level: Intermediate

Materials

❑ 7-count plastic canvas:
   ¼ sheet clear
   ¼ sheet dark green
   90 x 4-hole strip almond
❑ 2 (4-inch) plastic canvas circles
❑ Uniek Needloft plastic canvas yarn as listed in color key
❑ Kreinik Heavy (#32) Braid as listed in color key
❑ DMC size 5 pearl cotton as listed in color key
❑ Beading thread
❑ Clear monofilament thread
❑ Mill Hill glass seed beads:
   22 white #00479
   44 yellow creme #02002
❑ Mill Hill glass pebble beads:
   2 crystal #05161
   15 amethyst #05202

❑ Beading needle
❑ #16 tapestry needle
❑ 4-inch (10.2cm) or longer doll needle
❑ Cotton-tipped swab
❑ Thick white craft glue

Stitching Step by Step

Cutting

1 Cut two flower blossoms from clear plastic canvas and two flower leaves sections from dark green plastic canvas according to graphs.

2 Cut beaded edging strip from almond plastic canvas; cut plastic canvas circles to form rings.

Central Motif

1 Stitch both blossoms according to graph, filling in uncoded areas with orchid Continental Stitches.

2 Stitch leaves sections according to graph.

3 When the background stitching is complete, add embroidery stitches as follows:

Rose quartz heavy (#32) braid—Straight Stitch blossom petals.

Ultra dark pistachio green size 5 pearl cotton—Backstitch and Straight Stitch leaves.

4 Add bead clusters to blossom centers, threading on one yellow creme seed bead, one white seed bead, and another yellow creme seed bead for each cluster.

5 Whipstitch the leaf sections together where indicated on graph using emerald heavy (#32) braid.

6 Sandwich the unstitched blossom area of the leaves section between the stitched blossoms. Beginning near the lower edge of the blossom, Whipstitch all four layers together along one red Whipstitch line at the edge of the blossom; stop.

7 Using emerald heavy (#32) braid, Straight Stitch down flower stem, coming out the lower end of the bottom flower petal, down the stem, through the last hole at the bottom of the stem, and back up the other side before again burying the end of the braid on the wrong side of the bottom petal.

8 Resume Whipstitching all layers together around the edges of the blossom using rose quartz heavy (#32) braid.

Outer Ring

Join the almond beaded edging strip to the rings using lilac heavy (#32) braid.

Assembly

Suspend the flower in the ring, threading one crystal pebble bead onto the clear thread at the top of the flower and one crystal pebble bead at the bottom of the flower.

Finishing

1 Overcast the inner edge of the ring using eggshell yarn.

2 Attach hanging loop.

3 Glue an amethyst pebble bead to each bead placement bar on the edging strip, drawing the hanging loop through the pebble bead at the top of the spinner.

Flower Blossom
17 holes x 15 holes
Cut 2 from clear plastic canvas

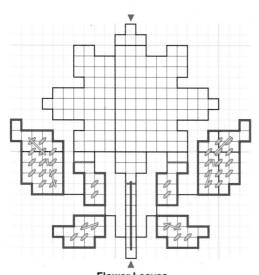

Flower Leaves
23 holes x 22 holes
Cut 2 from dark green plastic canvas,
cutting away blue lines

COLOR KEY	
Yards	**Plastic Canvas Yarn**
2 (1.8m)	▨ Fern #23
3 (2.7m)	☐ Eggshell #39
2 (1.8m)	▨ Lilac #45
2 (1.8m)	Uncoded areas on blossoms are orchid #44 Continental Stitches
	Heavy (#32) Braid
4 (3.7m)	✎ Emerald #009 Straight Stitch
4 (3.7m)	Lilac #023
5 (4.6m)	✎ Rose quartz #3237 Straight Stitch and Whipstitch
	Size 5 Pearl Cotton
1 (0.9m)	✎ Ultra dark pistachio green #890 Backstitch and Straight Stitch
	● Bead cluster placement
	✎ Whipstitch line

Color numbers given are for Uniek Needloft plastic canvas yarn, Kreinik Heavy (#32) Braid and DMC size 5 pearl cotton.

Lighthouse

Size: 5½ inches (14cm) in diameter
Skill Level: Intermediate

Materials

- ❏ 7-count plastic canvas:
  - ¼ sheet clear
  - 90 x 4-hole strip white
- ❏ 2 (4-inch) plastic canvas circles
- ❏ Uniek Needloft plastic canvas yarn as listed in color key
- ❏ Kreinik Heavy (#32) Braid as listed in color key
- ❏ DMC size 5 pearl cotton as listed in color key
- ❏ Clear monofilament thread
- ❏ Mill Hill glass seed beads:
  - 3 crystal #00161
- ❏ Mill Hill glass pebble beads:
  - 2 crystal #05161
  - 15 silver #05021
- ❏ Beading needle
- ❏ #16 tapestry needle

- ❏ 4-inch (10.2cm) or longer doll needle
- ❏ Cotton-tipped swab
- ❏ Toothpick or straight pin (optional)
- ❏ Thick white craft glue

Stitching Step by Step

Cutting

1 Cut one lighthouse A and one lighthouse B from clear plastic canvas according to graphs.

2 Cut beaded edging strip from white plastic canvas; cut plastic canvas circles to form rings.

Central Motif

1 Stitch both lighthouses according to graphs, filling in uncoded areas with white Continental Stitches.

2 When the background stitching is complete, add embroidery stitches as follows:

White yarn—Referring to stitch diagram on page 10, work Smyrna Cross Stitch in light at top of lighthouse.

Black yarn—Straight Stitch diagonal stripes on lighthouse tower and vertical stitches for door and windows on workroom.

Black size 5 pearl cotton—Straight Stitch details indicated by green lines on graphs.

3 Whipstitch the lighthouses together along the roofline using black yarn; add a French Knot at the top edge, wrapping the yarn around the needle once. Complete Whipstitching using gray yarn and blue zircon heavy (#32) braid according to graphs.

4 Work additional embroidery stitches as follows:

Black size 5 pearl cotton—Straight Stitch details indicated by purple lines on graphs over Whipstitched edge.

Outer Ring
Join the white beaded edging strip to the rings using gunmetal heavy (#32) braid.

Assembly
Suspend the lighthouse in the ring, threading one crystal pebble bead and three crystal seed beads onto the clear thread at the top of the lighthouse (with seed beads adjacent to roof), and one crystal pebble bead at the bottom of the lighthouse.

Finishing
1 Overcast the inner edge of the ring using white yarn.

2 Attach hanging loop.

3 Glue a silver pebble bead to each bead placement bar on the edging strip, drawing the hanging loop through the pebble bead at the top of the spinner.

Option: *Using a toothpick or straight pin, apply tiny drops of glue to the black diagonal stripes to space them evenly and hold them more securely in place.*

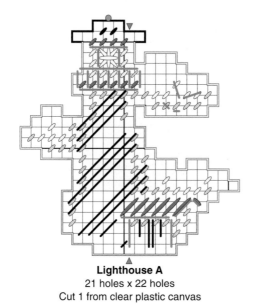

Lighthouse A
21 holes x 22 holes
Cut 1 from clear plastic canvas

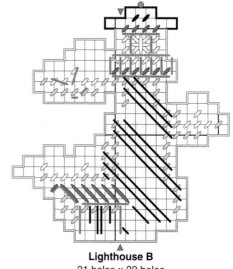

Lighthouse B
21 holes x 22 holes
Cut 1 from clear plastic canvas

COLOR KEY

Yards	Plastic Canvas Yarn
3 (2.7m)	■ Black #00
1 (0.9m)	▨ Red #01
3 (2.7m)	▨ Silver #37
1 (0.9m)	□ Eggshell #39
6 (5.5m)	Uncoded areas on lighthouse are White #41 Continental Stitches
	✿ White #41 Smyrna Cross Stitch
	╱ Black #00 Straight Stitch
	● Black #00 French Knot
	Heavy (#32) Metallic Braid
4 (3.7m)	Gunmetal #011HL
	Heavy (#32) Braid
2 (1.8m)	╱ Blue zircon #3214 Whipstitch
	Size 5 Pearl Cotton
2 (1.8m)	╱ Black #310 Straight Stitch

Color numbers given are for Uniek Needloft plastic canvas yarn, Kreinik heavy (#32) braid and DMC size 5 pearl cotton.

House

Size: 5½ inches (14cm) in diameter
Skill Level: Intermediate

Materials

❑ 7-count plastic canvas:
  ¼ sheet clear
  90 x 4-hole strip almond
❑ 2 (4-inch) plastic canvas circles
❑ Uniek Needloft plastic canvas yarn as listed in color key
❑ Kreinik Medium (#16) Braid as listed in color key
❑ Kreinik Heavy (#32) Braid as listed in color key
❑ DMC size 3 pearl cotton as listed in color key
❑ DMC size 5 pearl cotton as listed in color key
❑ 2 yards (1.8m) bead thread
❑ Clear monofilament thread
❑ Mill Hill glass seed beads:
  42 Christmas red #00165
  54 Royal plum #02012
❑ Mill Hill glass pebble beads:
  2 crystal #05161
  15 old gold #05557
❑ Beading needle
❑ #16 tapestry needle
❑ 4-inch (10.2cm) or longer doll needle
❑ Cotton-tipped swab
❑ Thick white craft glue

Stitching Step by Step

Cutting

1 Cut one house A and one house B from clear plastic canvas according to graphs.

2 Cut beaded edging strip from almond plastic canvas; cut plastic canvas circles to form rings.

Central Motif

1 Stitch both houses according to graphs, filling in uncoded areas with beige Continental Stitches.

2 When the background stitching is complete, add embroidery stitches as follows:

Ultra dark beaver gray size 5 pearl cotton—Backstitch and Straight Stitch windows, doors and walls.

White size 3 pearl cotton—Straight Stitch windows and doors; form French Knots at corners, wrapping pearl cotton around needle twice.

1 ply separated from a strand of beige yarn—French Knot doorknobs, wrapping yarn around needle once.

Peridot medium (#16) braid—Backstitch leaves on window boxes.

3 Add bead clusters to window boxes, threading on three Christmas red seed beads or three royal plum seed beads for each cluster, according to graphs.

4 Whipstitch the houses together using black and beige yarns, and peridot medium (#16) braid according to graphs.

Outer Ring

Join the almond beaded edging strip to the rings using curry heavy (#32) braid.

Assembly

Suspend the house in the ring, threading one crystal pebble bead onto the clear thread at the top of the house, and one at the bottom of the house.

Finishing

1 Overcast the inner edge of the ring using eggshell yarn.

2 Attach hanging loop.

3 Glue an old gold pebble bead to each bead placement bar on the edging strip, drawing the hanging loop through the pebble bead at the top of the spinner.

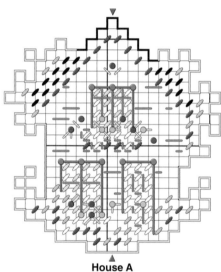

House A
21 holes x 22 holes
Cut 1 from clear plastic canvas

House B
21 holes x 22 holes
Cut 1 from clear plastic canvas

COLOR KEY

Yards	Plastic Canvas Yarn
2 (1.8m)	■ Black #00
2 (1.8m)	▨ Fern #23
1 (0.9m)	▨ Christmas green #28
1 (0.9m)	▨ Baby blue #36
2 (1.8m)	Eggshell #39
2 (1.8m)	□ White #41
1 (0.9m)	▨ Camel #43
5 (4.6m)	Uncoded areas on house are beige #40 Continental Stitches
	╱ Beige #40 Whipstitch
	● Beige #40 1-ply French Knot (1 wrap)
Medium (#16) Braid	
6 (5.5m)	╱ Peridot #3215 Backstitch
Heavy (#32) Braid	
4 (3.7m)	Curry #2122
Size 3 Pearl Cotton	
	╱ White Straight Stitch
2 (1.8m)	● White French Knot (2 wraps)
Size 5 Pearl Cotton	
2 (1.8m)	╱ Ultra dark beaver gray #844 Backstitch and Straight Stitch
Bead Cluster Placement	
	● Christmas red
	● Royal plum

Color numbers given are for Uniek Needloft plastic canvas yarn; Kreinik Medium (#16) and Heavy (#32) Braids, and DMC size 3 and size 5 pearl cotton.

Hearts

Size: 5½ inches (14cm) in diameter
Skill Level: Intermediate

Materials

❑ 7-count white plastic canvas:
  ¼ sheet
  90 x 4-hole strip
❑ 2 (4-inch) plastic canvas circles
❑ Uniek Needloft plastic canvas yarn as listed in color key
❑ Kreinik Heavy (#32) Braid as listed in color key
❑ Clear monofilament thread
❑ Mill Hill glass pebble beads:
  3 crystal #05161
  19 ruby #05025
❑ Mill Hill glass seed beads:
  14 crystal #00161
❑ #16 tapestry needle
❑ 4-inch (10.2cm) or longer doll needle

❑ Beading needle
❑ Cotton-tipped swab
❑ Thick white craft glue

Stitching Step by Step

Cutting

1 Cut two hearts motifs from white plastic canvas according to graph. Carefully cut off the bead placement bars (shaded yellow on graph) on one of the heart motifs. (The pebble beads will not fit over doubled bars of plastic canvas.)

2 Cut beaded edging strip from white plastic canvas; cut plastic canvas circles to form rings.

Central Motif

1 Complete yarn Continental Stitches on both hearts motifs according to graph.

2 Whipstitch the motifs together around the individual hearts using ruby heavy (#32) braid.

Outer Ring

Join the white beaded edging strip to the rings using red heavy (#32) braid.

Assembly

1 Draw the doll needle between plastic canvas layers from the top center point of the heart motif. As the needle tip emerges in the center opening, thread a crystal pebble bead onto the needle; continue drawing the needle between the plastic canvas layers until the needle tip extends slightly beyond the bottom edge of the heart motif; set aside.

2 Suspend the hearts motif in the ring as directed in General Instructions (page 1), threading one crystal pebble bead and seven crystal seed beads onto the clear thread at the top of the hearts motif. Thread the ends of the clear thread into the eye of the doll needle and pull through the center of the hearts motif, catching the crystal pebble bead in the center. Thread seven crystal seed beads and one crystal pebble bead onto the clear thread at the bottom of the hearts motif before securing the thread ends at the bottom of the ring.

```
COLOR KEY
Yards        Plastic Canvas Yarn
3 (2.7m)  ■ Red #01
2 (1.8m)  □ Christmas red #02
2 (1.8m)    White #41
             Heavy (#32) Braid
4 (3.7m)     Red #003
5 (4.6m)  ╱ Ruby #061 Overcasting
Color numbers given are for Uniek Needloft plastic
canvas yarn and Kreinik Heavy (#32) Braid.
```

Finishing

1 Overcast the inner edge of the ring using white yarn.

2 Attach hanging loop.

3 Glue a ruby pebble bead to each bead placement bar on the edging strip, drawing the hanging loop through the pebble bead at the top of the spinner.

4 Glue a ruby pebble bead to each bead placement bar on the central hearts motif.

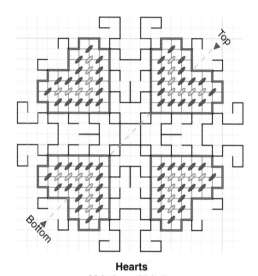

Hearts
22 holes x 22 holes
Cut 2 from white plastic canvas,
cutting away blue lines

Cross

Size: 5½ inches (14cm) in diameter
Skill Level: Intermediate

Materials

❑ 7-count almond plastic canvas:
  ¼ sheet
  90 x 4-hole strip
❑ 2 (4-inch) plastic canvas circles
❑ Uniek Needloft plastic canvas yarn as listed in color key
❑ Kreinik Heavy (#32) Braid as listed in color key
❑ Clear monofilament thread
❑ Mill Hill glass pebble beads:
  17 crystal #05161
❑ #16 tapestry needle
❑ 4-inch (10.2cm) or longer doll needle
❑ Cotton-tipped swab
❑ Thick white craft glue

Stitching Step by Step

Cutting

1 Cut two crosses and two cross backing pieces from almond plastic canvas according to graphs.

2 Cut beaded edging strip from almond plastic canvas; cut plastic canvas circles to form rings.

Central Motif

1 Stitch both crosses according to graph.

2 When the background stitching is complete, Backstitch and Straight Stitch crosses using cat's eye heavy (#32) braid.

3 Sandwich the unstitched cross backing sections between the stitched crosses, aligning the Whipstitching lines highlighted in red. Whipstitch to join all layers along these lines using cat's eye heavy (#32) braid.

Outer Ring

Join the almond beaded edging strip to the rings using cat's eye heavy (#32) braid.

Assembly

Suspend the cross in the ring, threading one crystal pebble bead onto the clear thread at the top of the cross and one crystal pebble bead at the bottom of the cross.

Finishing

1 Overcast the inner edge of the ring using eggshell yarn.

2 Attach hanging loop.

3 Glue a crystal pebble bead to each bead placement bar on the edging strip, drawing the hanging loop through the pebble bead at the top of the spinner.

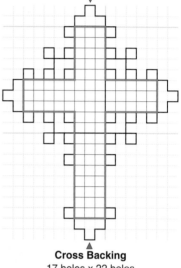

COLOR KEY		
Yards	**Plastic Canvas Yarn**	
4 (3.7m)	▢ Eggshell #39	
	Heavy (#32) Braid	
7 (6.4m)	⧄ Cat's eye #3202 Backstitch, Straight Stitch and Whipstitch	
	⧄ Whipstitch	
Color numbers given are for Uniek Needloft plastic canvas yarn and Kreinik Heavy (#32) Braid.		

Cross
13 holes x 18 holes
Cut 2 from clear plastic canvas

Cross Backing
17 holes x 22 holes
Cut 2 from almond plastic canvas,
cutting away blue lines

Sun

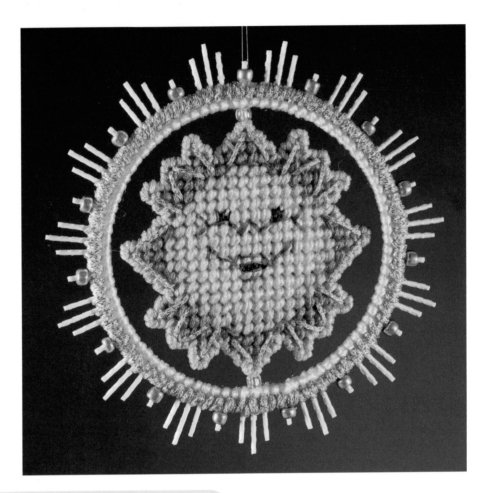

Size: 5½ inches (14cm) in diameter
Skill Level: Intermediate

Materials

❏ 7-count plastic canvas:
  ¼ sheet clear
  90 x 4-hole strip white
❏ 2 (4-inch) plastic canvas circles
❏ Uniek Needloft plastic canvas yarn as listed in
  color key
❏ Kreinik Heavy (#32) Braid as listed in color key
❏ DMC 6-strand cotton embroidery floss as listed
  in color key
❏ Clear monofilament thread
❏ Mill Hill glass pebble beads:
  2 crystal #05161
  15 old gold #05557
❏ #16 tapestry needle
❏ 4-inch (10.2cm) or longer doll needle
❏ Cotton-tipped swab
❏ Thick white craft glue

Stitching Step by Step

Cutting

1 Cut two suns from clear plastic canvas according to graph.

2 Cut beaded edging strip from white plastic canvas; cut plastic canvas circles to form rings.

Central Motif

1 Stitch both suns according to graph, filling in uncoded areas with yellow Continental Stitches.

2 When the background stitching is complete, add embroidery stitches as follows:

Black yarn—Straight Stitch mouth.
1 ply separated from a strand of white yarn—Backstitch a tiny highlight in each eye.
Heliodor heavy (#32) braid—Straight Stitch sun's rays.
4 strands separated from a length of ultra very dark topaz embroidery floss—Backstitch and Straight Stitch remaining facial details.

3 Whipstitch the suns together using light peach heavy (#32) braid.

Outer Ring

Join the white beaded edging strip to the rings using heliodor heavy (#32) braid.

Assembly

Suspend the sun in the ring, threading one crystal pebble bead onto the clear thread at the top of the sun, and one at the bottom of the sun.

Finishing

1 Overcast the inner edge of the ring using white yarn.

2 Attach hanging loop.

3 Glue an old gold pebble bead to each bead placement bar on the edging strip, drawing the hanging loop through the pebble bead at the top of the spinner.

COLOR KEY	
Yards	**Plastic Canvas Yarn**
1 (0.9m)	■ Black #00
3 (2.7m)	▨ Rust #09
2 (1.8m)	☐ Tangerine #11
4 (3.7m)	Uncoded area on sun is yellow #57 Continental Stitches
	✦ Black #00 Straight Stitch
3 (2.7m)	✧ White #41 1-ply Backstitch
Heavy (#32) Braid	
6 (5.5m)	✦ Heliodor #3221 Straight Stitch
4 (3.7m)	✦ Light peach #9192 Whipstitch
6-Strand Embroidery Floss	
2 (1.8m)	✦ Ultra very dark topaz #780 4-strand Backstitch and Straight Stitch

Color numbers given are for Uniek Needloft plastic canvas yarn, Kreinik Heavy (#32) Braid and DMC 6-strand cotton embroidery floss.

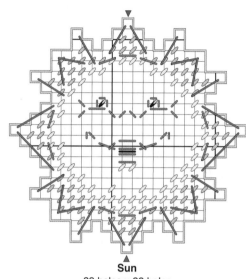

Sun
23 holes x 22 holes
Cut 2 from clear plastic canvas

Moon

Size: 5½ inches (14cm) in diameter
Skill Level: Intermediate

Materials

❏ 7-count plastic canvas:
  ¼ sheet clear
  90 x 4-hole strip white
❏ 2 (4-inch) plastic canvas circles
❏ Uniek Needloft plastic canvas yarn as listed in color key
❏ Kreinik Heavy (#32) Braid as listed in color key
❏ DMC size 5 pearl cotton as listed in color key
❏ 2 yards (1.8m) bead thread
❏ Clear monofilament thread
❏ Mill Hill glass seed beads:
  35 crystal #00161
❏ Mill Hill glass pebble beads:
  2 crystal #05161
  22 silver #05021

❏ #16 tapestry needle
❏ Beading needle
❏ 4-inch (10.2cm) or longer doll needle
❏ Cotton-tipped swab
❏ Thick white craft glue

Stitching Step by Step

Cutting

1 Cut one moon A, one moon B and two stars from clear plastic canvas according to graphs.

2 Cut beaded edging strip from white plastic canvas; cut plastic canvas circles to form rings.

Moon

1 Stitch moons according to graphs, filling in uncoded areas with white Continental Stitches.

2 When the background stitching is complete, add embroidery stitches as follows:

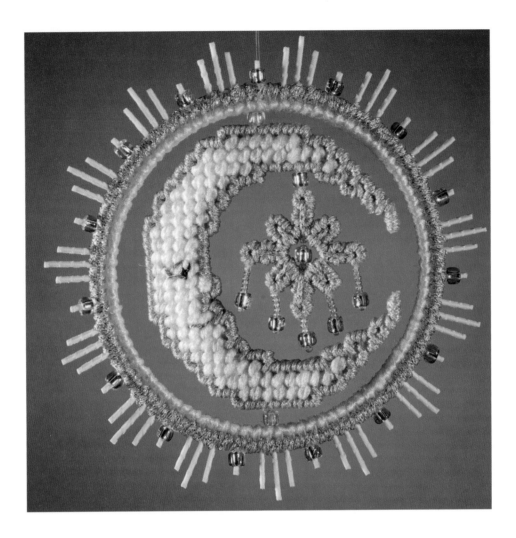

1 ply separated from a strand of white yarn—Backstitch a tiny highlight in each eye.

Medium brown gray size 5 pearl cotton—Backstitch and Straight Stitch eye details and short mouth line.

3 Whipstitch moons together along inner edge using star green heavy (#32) braid.

4 Work additional embroidery stitches as follows:

Full strand of white yarn—Backstitch nose.

Medium brown gray size 5 pearl cotton—Straight Stitch diagonal mouth line over Whipstitched edge.

5 Whipstitch moons together along remaining edges using star green heavy (#32) braid.

Stitch Star

1 Whipstitch stars together using star green heavy (#32) braid.

2 Add embroidery stitches as follows:

Brazilianite heavy (#32) braid—Straight Stitch star's rays, bringing the braid through the Whipstitched edge of the center opening, through the tip of the star, and back into the Whipstitched edge at the original point.

Bead Star

1 Thread beading needle with a single strand of clear monofilament thread. Position star on a point. Anchor the thread end in the star and emerge at one of the outermost fringe placement points.

2 String six crystal seed beads, one silver pebble bead, and one crystal seed bead onto clear monofilament thread. Thread the needle back through the beads, skipping the final seed bead and passing the needle through the silver pebble bead and the first six crystal seed beads. Draw up the excess thread so that the fringe dangles freely.

3 Take the threaded needle back through stitching, emerging at the next fringe attachment point. Thread five crystal seed beads, one silver pebble bead, and one crystal seed bead onto the needle. Draw needle back through fringe as in step 2.

4 Skipping the center bottom ray, take the threaded needle back through the stitching and add fringe to the remaining rays to match the first two. Anchor the thread end in the stitching and trim.

5 Thread a single crystal seed bead onto a length of clear thread, centering the bead on the thread. Thread both ends of the thread in the beading needle; thread on one silver pebble bead and four crystal seed beads.

6 Insert the needle between the plastic canvas layers at the tip of the center bottom ray. When the needle reaches the star's center opening, thread on two crystal seed beads, one silver pebble bead and two more crystal seed beads.

7 Draw the needle straight up through the star, between plastic canvas layers. When the needle emerges from the top tip of the star, thread on one silver pebble bead. Draw up the extra thread so that the fringe dangles from the bottom and the beads in the center and at the top of the star are aligned.

8 Attach the beaded star to the moon where indicated on the moon graphs. Anchor the thread end in the stitching and trim.

Outer Ring

Join the white beaded edging strip to the rings using Brazilianite heavy (#32) braid.

Assembly

Referring to the General Instructions for "Assembly" (page 2), suspend the moon in the ring, but attach the top and bottom with separate strands of clear thread; do not run thread through the center. Thread one crystal pebble bead onto the clear thread at the top of the moon, and one at the bottom of the moon.

Finishing

1 Overcast the inner edge of the ring using white yarn.

2 Attach hanging loop.

3 Glue a silver pebble bead to each bead placement bar on the edging strip, drawing the hanging loop through the pebble bead at the top of the spinner.

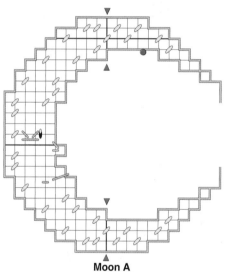

Moon A
21 holes x 22 holes
Cut 1 from clear plastic canvas

COLOR KEY

Yards	Plastic Canvas Yarn
1 (0.9m)	■ Black #00
2 (1.8m)	☐ Baby blue #36
5 (4.6m)	Uncoded areas on moons are white #41 Continental Stitches
	╱ White #41 1-ply Backstitch
	╱ White #41 full-strand Backstitch and Straight Stitch
	Heavy (#32) Braid
4 (3.7m)	╱ Brazilianite #3232 Straight Stitch
6 (5.5m)	╱ Star green #9194 Whipstitch
	Size 5 Pearl Cotton
1 (0.9m)	╱ Medium brown gray #3022 Backstitch and Straight Stitch
	● Fringe placement
	● Attach star to moon

Color numbers given are for Uniek Needloft plastic canvas yarn, Kreinik Heavy (#32) Braid and DMC size 5 pearl cotton.

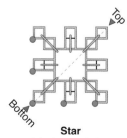

Star
7 holes x 7 holes
Cut 2 from clear plastic canvas

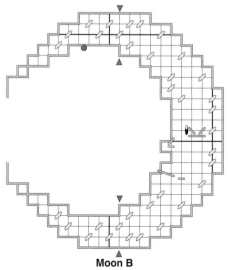

Moon B
21 holes x 22 holes
Cut 1 from clear plastic canvas

Sunflower

Size: 5½ inches (14cm) in diameter
Skill Level: Intermediate

Materials
❑ 7-count plastic canvas:
    ¼ sheet clear
    90 x 4-hole strip almond
❑ 2 (4-inch) plastic canvas circles
❑ Uniek Needloft plastic canvas yarn as listed in individual color keys
❑ Kreinik Heavy (#32) Braid as listed in color key
❑ DMC size 5 pearl cotton as listed in color key
❑ 2 yards (1.8m) bead thread
❑ Clear monofilament thread
❑ Mill Hill glass seed beads:
    84 pale peach #00148
    168 Victorian gold #02011
❑ Mill Hill glass pebble beads:
    2 crystal #05161
    15 old gold #05557
❑ #16 tapestry needle
❑ Beading needle
❑ 4-inch (10.2cm) or longer doll needle
❑ Cotton-tipped swab
❑ Thick white craft glue

Stitching Step by Step

Cutting
1 Cut two sunflowers from clear plastic canvas according to graph.

2 Cut beaded edging strip from almond plastic canvas; cut plastic canvas circles to form rings.

Central Motif
1 Stitch both sunflowers according to graph, filling in uncoded areas with yellow Continental Stitches.

2 When the background stitching is complete, add embroidery stitches to both sunflowers as follows:

Black size 5 pearl cotton—Straight Stitch sunflower center.
Dark beige brown size 5 pearl cotton—Backstitch and Straight Stitch petals.

3 Add bead clusters to sunflowers, threading on one Victorian gold seed bead, one pale peach seed bead, and another Victorian gold seed bead for each cluster.

4 Whipstitch the sunflowers together using star yellow heavy (#32) braid.

Outer Ring
Join the beaded edging strip to the rings using copper hi-lustre heavy (#32) braid.

Assembly
Suspend the sunflower in the ring, threading one crystal pebble bead onto the clear thread at the top of the sunflower, and one at the bottom of the sunflower.

Finishing
1 Overcast the inner edge of the ring using eggshell yarn.

2 Attach hanging loop.

3 Glue an old gold pebble bead to each bead placement bar on the edging strip, drawing the hanging loop through the pebble bead at the top of the spinner.

```
COLOR KEY
Yards       Plastic Canvas Yarn
1 (0.9m)  □ Rust #09
2 (1.8m)  ▨ Tangerine #11
3 (2.7m)  ▨ Cinnamon #14
1 (0.9m)  ■ Brown #15
2 (1.8m)    Eggshell #39
4 (3.7m)    Uncoded area on sunflower is
            yellow #57 Continental Stitches
            Heavy (#32) Braid
4 (3.7m)    Copper hi lustre #021HL
6 (5.5m)  ╱ Star yellow #091 Whipstitch
            Size 5 Pearl Cotton
1 (0.9m)  ╱ Black #310 Straight Stitch
3 (2.7m)  ╱ Dark beige brown #839
            Backstitch and Straight Stitch
          ○ Bead cluster placement
Color numbers given are for Uniek Needloft plastic
canvas yarn, Kreinik Heavy (#32) Braid and DMC
size 5 pearl cotton.
```

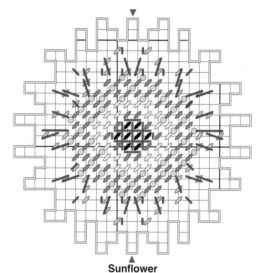

Sunflower
23 holes x 22 holes
Cut 2 from clear plastic canvas

306 E. Parr Road
Berne, IN 46711
www.NeedlecraftShop.com
© 2006 The Needlecraft Shop

The full line of The Needlecraft Shop
products is carried by Annie's Attic catalog.

TOLL-FREE ORDER LINE
or to request a free catalog
(800) 582-6643
Customer Service
(800) 449-0440
Fax (800) 882-6643
Visit www.AnniesAttic.com

ISBN: 1-57367-221-1

All rights reserved.

Printed in USA

1 2 3 4 5 6 7 8 9

Shopping for Supplies

For supplies, first shop your local craft
and needlework stores. Some supplies
may be found in fabric, hardware and
discount stores. If you are unable to find
the supplies you need, please call Annie's
Attic at (800) 259-4000 to request a free
catalog that sells plastic canvas supplies.

Getting Started

Before You Cut

Buy one brand of canvas for each entire project, as brands can differ slightly in the distance between bars. Count holes carefully from the graph before you cut, using the bolder lines that show each 10 holes. These 10-mesh lines begin in the lower left corner of each graph to make counting easier. Mark canvas before cutting, then remove all marks completely before stitching. If the piece is cut in a rectangular or square shape and is either not worked, or worked with only one color and one type of stitch, we do not include the graph in the pattern. Instead, we give the cutting and stitching instructions in the general instructions or with the individual project instructions.

Covering the Canvas

Bring needle up from back of work, leaving a short length of yarn on back of canvas; work over short length to secure. To end a thread, weave needle and thread through the wrong side of your last few stitches; clip. Follow the numbers on the small graphs beside each stitch illustration; bring your needle up from the back of the work on odd numbers and down through the front of the work on even numbers. Work embroidery stitches last, after the canvas has been completely covered by the needlepoint stitches.

Basic Stitches

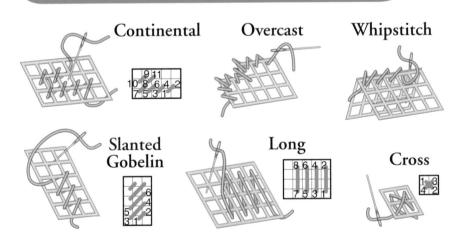

Continental

Overcast

Whipstitch

Slanted Gobelin

Long

Cross

Embroidery Stitches

French Knot

Lazy Daisy

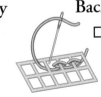

Backstitch

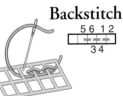

Straight

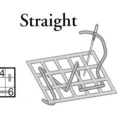

METRIC KEY:
millimeters = (mm)
centimeters = (cm)
meters = (m)
grams = (g)